SECRET LIVES OF

DEEP-SEA CREATURES

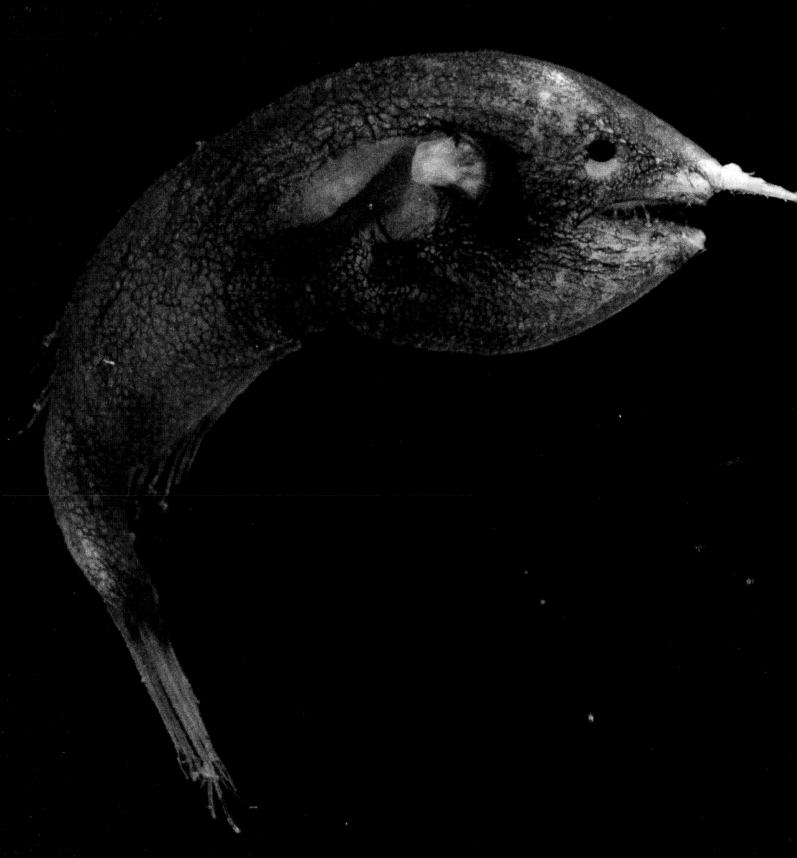

SECRET LIVES OF
DEEP-SEA CREATURES

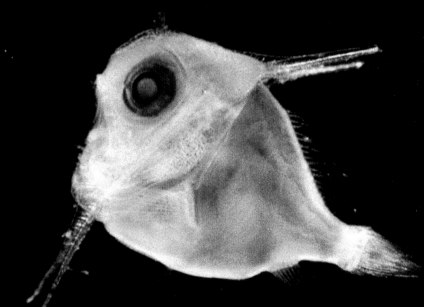

SARA SWAN MILLER

Marshall Cavendish
Benchmark
New York

The author and publisher would like to thank Sidney Horenstein, Geologist and Environmental Educator Emeritus, for his generous assistance in reading the manuscript.

EDITOR: JOYCE STANTON   PUBLISHER: MICHELLE BISSON
ART DIRECTOR: ANAHID HAMPARIAN   SERIES DESIGNER: KRISTEN BRANCH

Photo research by Laurie Platt Winfrey, Carousel Research
Cover: Visuals Unlimited/ E. Widder The Photographs in this book are used by permission and through the courtesy of: *Animals/Animals:* OSF/ Scripps Institute of Oceanography, 33; Bob Cranston, 36; OSF/R. Jackman, 38. *Peter Arnold:* Mirko Zanni, 25; Christian Leroy/ Biosphoto, 45. *Getty Images:* Hulton, 11; RF/Comstock, 19; Clive Bromhall/Photolibrary, Back cover + 29; Jeff Rotman/Image Bank, 43 bottom. *Minden Pictures:* Norbert Wu, Titlepage, 16, 26. *National Geographic Images:* Brian J. Skerry, Half title, 34; Emory Krisof, 14, 31; Norbert Wu/Minden Pictures, 20 ; Ingo Arndt/Minden Pictures, 23. *Photo Researchers:* Science Source, 13; Richard Ellis, 30. *Visuals Unlimited:* E. Widder/HBOI, 8, 43 top; David Wrobel, 24; David Fleetham, 40.

Printed in Malaysia (T)
135642

Front cover: The unusual red light organs on this dragonfish place it in a species of its own.
Half-title page: A giant squid hunts for its dinner.
Title page: An anglerfish lures its prey with the lighted tip of its long, bony rod.
Back cover: Two males feed off a female anglerfish.

CONTENTS

A fierce predator, the anglerfish is one of the many strange creatures that make their lives in the deep.

STRANGE CREATURES
OF THE

FOR THOUSANDS OF YEARS, people have wondered what lives in the dark depths of the ocean. They have told tales of giant sea monsters that could gobble up a whale in one bite. They have imagined huge sea dragons lurking in the deep waters, ready to lunge up and devour fishermen sailing along on the surface. They have drawn pictures of fantastic creatures like a monster octopus wrapping its arms around a sailing ship, about to drag it down into the cold, dark depths.

For all those years, though, people could only imagine what lived deep in the sea. There was no way for them to dive down far enough to find out. Even pearl divers could go no deeper than 100 feet (30 meters) without running out of breath.

Then, in 1872, the British ship *Challenger* set forth on a three-and-a-half-year voyage to explore the ocean depths. As the ship steamed around the world, the crew members collected specimens in large nets and sent **dredges** down on long lines to scoop up creatures miles below. They discovered four thousand new **species**. They did not, however, discover any sea monsters.

After the voyage of the *Challenger*, many other vessels set sail to sample the creatures of the deep. But there were drawbacks to using nets and dredges. The animals they brought up were dead by the time they got to the surface, and there was no way of knowing what those creatures' lives in the ocean were like. What the researchers needed was a way to go down into the ocean and see things with their own eyes. But

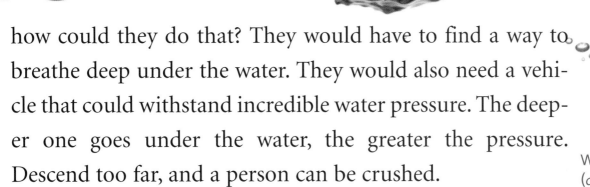

how could they do that? They would have to find a way to breathe deep under the water. They would also need a vehicle that could withstand incredible water pressure. The deeper one goes under the water, the greater the pressure. Descend too far, and a person can be crushed.

In 1930, William Beebe and Otis Barton began testing an underwater vehicle that solved those two problems. The bathysphere was a hollow steel ball with two thick windows made of quartz, a clear, hard mineral. It was lowered from a ship on a long steel cable. The walls and windows were designed to withstand high pressure. There were two oxygen tanks on board to supply air for the vehicle's two passengers. Beebe and Barton made thirty-two dives in the bathysphere, using a bright light

William Beebe (*center*) and members of his team with their famous invention, the bathysphere

to spot the underwater creatures. Their deepest dive was 3,028 feet (923 meters).

After the success of the bathysphere, other types of deep-sea vehicles, or submersibles, were invented. The first was the bathyscaphe. Shaped like a cylinder, or tube, this submersible could propel itself through the water. In 1960, a bathyscaphe called the *Trieste* dived down to the bottom of the Mariana Trench in the Pacific Ocean, the deepest-known spot on the planet. The ship reached a record-breaking depth of nearly 36,000 feet (10,970 meters).

Since then, divers have been exploring the deep in smaller submersibles, including the three-person *Alvin*. Researchers on the *Alvin* have spotted some fascinating creatures living around the **hydrothermal vents** on the ocean floor. These vents, also called hot vents, are created when seawater seeps through cracks in the earth's crust. The water, which has been heated to incredibly high temperatures by volcanic rock beneath the surface, bursts up like a geyser. The temperature around the vents can be hotter than 660 degrees Fahrenheit (350 degrees Celsius)! Yet all kinds of creatures, including huge tube worms and giant clams, thrive there in great numbers.

Most of us imagine the ocean floor as one large, flat expanse. Just like the land above the sea, however, the ocean floor has its own physical features. Around each of the earth's continents is a relatively shallow area known as the continental shelf. This shelf drops off at the continental slope, which descends to the broadest, flattest part of the ocean floor, the abyssal (uh-BISS-el) plain. Even here, the floor is not simply flat. The abyssal plain is dotted with thousands of small hills. In some areas, long trenches plunge to the very deepest depths of the ocean. The ocean floor also has its own interconnected system of mountain ranges, called mid-ocean ridges. The mid-ocean ridge system stretches more than 40,000

Superhot water, loaded with minerals, spews from hydrothermal vents on the ocean floor.

A REALLY LONG MOUNTAIN RANGE

The Mid-Atlantic Ridge is the longest mountain chain in the world—about 10,000 miles (16,000 kilometers) in all. That is more than twice as long as the Andes, the longest mountain chain on land.

miles (64,000 kilometers) as it wanders over the globe.

LIFE AT THE TOP

Scientists divide the ocean depths into zones. Each zone has its own special characteristics and its own special animal life. The top zone is called the epipelagic (eh-pih-puh-LAH-jik) zone. It goes from the surface down to 660 feet (200 meters). Just under the surface, the light is still bright, but as we descend, it begins to fade. At 330 feet (100 meters), 99 percent of the surface light is gone. Most of the color spectrum is gone, too, except for the blue spectrum. At this depth, the water is bathed in a dim blue light.

While the light is fading, the water pressure is increasing. At the very bottom of the epipelagic zone, the pressure is 294 pounds per square inch (20 atmospheres). That is already twenty times the pressure at the surface. The creatures that live in the epipelagic zone are familiar to anyone who has spent any time on the ocean. They include manta rays, sharks, dolphins, and most of the fish we eat: swordfish, tuna, flounder, sea bass, and so on.

GOING DEEPER . . .

Next comes the mesopelagic (meh-zuh-puh-LAH-jik) zone, or "middle sea." This zone goes from 660 feet (200 meters) down to 3,300 feet (1,000 meters). The top of this layer is a deep blue gloom. By 2,000 feet (610 meters), everything has become pitch-black. The water pressure increases greatly here. At the bottom of the zone, the pressure is one hundred times what it is on the surface.

Many of the creatures that live in the mesopelagic zone are

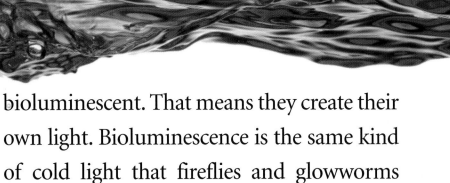

bioluminescent. That means they create their own light. Bioluminescence is the same kind of cold light that fireflies and glowworms produce. Deep-sea creatures use their light in various ways. Many use bioluminescence to find their way around and attract mates. Some use their light to lure prey. Others produce light to scare off predators. There is nothing like a sudden blinding flash to make a hunter back off! Lantern fish, hatchetfish, comb jellies, and dragonfish all make their home in the mesopelagic zone.

Creatures like this hatchetfish use their eyes and their bioluminescence to survive in the deep.

AND DEEPER . . .

Below the middle sea comes the bathypelagic (bah-thih-puh-LAH-jik) zone, or "deep sea." This zone begins at 3,300 feet (1,000 meters) and goes down to 13,000 feet (3,960 meters). There is no light here, and no way to tell the difference between

night and day. Many of the creatures have very small eyes. Since there is nothing to see, their eyes have simply **atrophied**.

Along with their tiny eyes, most of the creatures have large heads and mouths, which are equipped with sharp, curved-in teeth. These adaptations allow them to eat whatever comes near. There is not much to eat this far below the surface, so predators have to take what they can find. Anglerfish and some other deep-sea predators live and hunt down here full-time. Sperm whales dive down from the surface to hunt for food, but they have to swim all the way back up to breathe. Their bodies are adapted to withstand the drastic changes in water pressure. Down at the bottom of the bathypelagic zone, the pressure is 5,880 pounds per square inch (400 atmospheres). That's four hundred times greater than on the surface.

AND DEEPER STILL . . .

Going still deeper, we enter the abyssopelagic (uh-biss-oh-puh-LAH-jik) zone, or "bottomless sea." This zone stretches from 13,000 feet (3,960 meters) to 20,000 feet (6,100 meters). At the bottom, the pressure is an amazing 8,000 pounds per square inch (545 atmospheres).

It's hard to believe that anything can live down here. Yet some creatures do. Many are tiny, but some are much larger than similar creatures found in shallower waters. The giant squid, for instance, makes its home in this zone. It weighs more than 2,000 pounds (900 kilograms) and grows up to 46 feet (14 meters) long. Compare that to some squid in upper waters, which may be only 1 inch (2.5 centimeters) long.

At the Bottom of the World

The hadal (HAY-dull) zone is the deepest part of the ocean. It starts at 20,000 feet (6,100 meters) and descends to the ocean floor. In some places, it plunges into trenches nearly 36,000 feet (10,970 meters) deep. The word *hadal* comes from *Hades*, the name for the underworld in Greek myths.

The creatures that live in this deep, dark region are small.

Sea lilies look like plants, but they are really animals.

Some are black. Some are pale red, orange, or yellow. Others may have lost all their color and look dirty white or transparent. Not many creatures can stand the water pressure here. In the deepest part of the hadal zone, the pressure reaches an incredible 16,000 pounds per square inch (1,090 atmospheres). Yet a number of species have adapted to life at the bottom of the world. We can find sea lilies, sea spiders, and most abundant of all, sea cucumbers, which often rove along the seafloor in herds.

People have long been familiar with the creatures that live near the surface of the ocean. In this book, we will go deeper. Turn the page, and let's journey to the deepest, darkest parts of the ocean, in search of the secret lives of deep-sea creatures.

A lantern fish makes
a dash for safety from
the jaws of one of its
many predators, a
viper fish.

CREATURES OF THE MESOPELAGIC ZONE

660 TO 3,300 FEET
(200 TO 1,000 METERS)

LANTERN FISH

LANTERN FISH ARE very common in the mesopelagic zone. These fish are well named, because the photophores, or light organs, on their heads and bodies give off light like a lantern. Most of the photophores are on the lantern fish's back. These lights help the fish camouflage itself. When a predator looks up from below, the light from the photophores blends with the sunlight from above. That makes it very hard for the predator to see the lantern fish. Still, these bioluminescent creatures do have lots of enemies. All kinds of marine life, including tuna, mackerel, squid, seals, penguins, whales, and dolphins, like to dine on lantern fish.

Different species of lantern fish have different light patterns. This may help members of the same species recognize each other at breeding time. Some species, including Andersen's lantern fish, have two pairs of light organs on the head and body. These organs act like spotlights, helping the fish find its prey.

Lantern fish migrate, but not in the same way as birds. Instead of moving from north to south and back again every few months, they migrate up and down in the ocean depths each morning and evening. During the day, the fish rest in the mesopelagic zone. At night, they migrate up to the surface waters. There they get to work gobbling up tiny **crustaceans**, such as copepods and krill, with their bands of little sharp teeth. When dawn comes, the fish swim back down again.

Lantern fish live in warm oceans all around the globe, and

there are plenty of them. They make up 65 percent of all the fish in the mesopelagic zone.

COMB JELLIES

Comb jellies are also common in the middle sea. They might remind you of jellyfish, but the two creatures are not related. Comb jellies have eight comblike rows of ctenes (TEENZ), which are groups of slender fibers. They beat their ctenes to move themselves through the water. If you could see one of these creatures in the searchlights of an undersea vehicle, you would notice that the ctenes break up the light into a rainbow of rippling colors as the comb jelly shoots along.

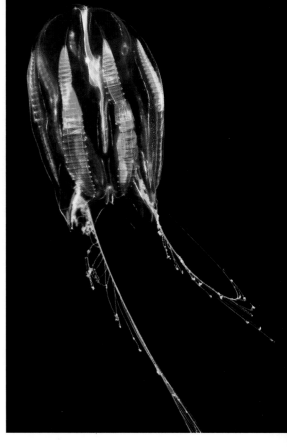

There are about 125 species of comb jellies, and all are hungry predators.

Comb jellies feed on **plankton**, the masses of tiny plants and animals that float in the sea. They especially like the **larvae** of mollusks, crabs, lobsters, and fish. Some comb jellies have sticky **tentacles** for capturing their prey. Others have large, fleshy lobes that make the creature look something like a catcher's mitt.

Some kinds of comb jellies, like this *Beroe abyssicola*, have no tentacles and simply swallow their prey whole. This kind of comb jelly feeds mostly on other comb jellies.

A few comb jellies do not have tentacles or lobes. They just open their gaping mouths and engulf their prey.

All comb jellies are beautiful, but the bloodybelly comb jelly is especially dazzling. Its body is deep red or purple, and in the light, the colors sparkle and shimmer. What good is the bloodybelly's deep red color? Many of the creatures that this comb jelly eats are bioluminescent. They keep glowing for a while after they are swallowed. If the comb jelly were not deeply colored, the light from its bioluminescent food would continue to show, making it an easy target for a predator.

DRAGONFISH

Dragonfish have big mouths filled with enormous fanglike teeth. Although these fish are small, they can be fierce predators, hunting down and devouring prey much larger than themselves. Special adaptations give them a remarkable edge

as hunters. Many species of dragonfish have hinged jaws that allow them to open their mouths really wide—some as wide as 180 degrees! Some species have hinged teeth, too. The teeth fold backward but not forward, so that when a tasty morsel is taken in, it can't slip back out.

With its many light organs glowing, the dragonfish certainly has a fearsome appearance.

Female dragonfish really deserve their name. Even though some are only 4 to 6 inches (10 to 15 centimeters) long, these ferocious predators manage to eat just about anything they find. Male dragonfish, on the other hand, are not fierce at all. They are only about 3 inches (8 centimeters) long, and they have no mouth or stomach, so they can't even eat. They seem to live only to mate with the females. After mating, they die.

There are about 250 species of dragonfish. They live in warm oceans all around the world. Since they live in deep waters, divers seldom meet up with one. That's a good thing, since a dragonfish could easily bite off a diver's foot!

An anglerfish
rests in wait for
a juicy morsel
to appear.

CREATURES OF THE
BATHYPELAGIC
ZONE

3,300 TO 13,000 FEET
(1,000 TO 3,960 METERS)

ANGLERFISH

ANGLERFISH ARE SOME OF the weirdest-looking fish in the ocean. The females have short, fat bodies and enormous heads. Their jellylike flesh wobbles when they move. Since they rest in wait for their prey, they don't need streamlined bodies to help them swim through the water.

Anglerfish are well adapted for life in the dark bathypelagic zone. The female has a bony rod growing on top of her head.

On the tip of the rod is a fleshy lure that lights up. Other fish are drawn to the light. When they come close, the anglerfish makes a grab for them. With her huge mouth, she can swallow most prey whole.

Besides having huge mouths, female anglerfish have very stretchy throats and stomachs. They can eat large prey, including fish longer than themselves. When these weird sea creatures have eaten, their great bulging stomachs make them look even stranger.

Anglerfish have odd mating habits, too. The males are much smaller and more streamlined than the females. Once they become adults, their digestive tracts start to **degenerate**. Soon they won't be able to eat on their own. So they begin to search the waters for a female. This isn't easy, because there are very few anglerfish in the depths. Luckily, males can sense chemicals in the water that help them track down a mate. When a male finds a female, he attaches himself and won't let go. Their bloodstreams join, and the male lives off the nutrients in the female's blood for the rest of his very short life.

When the female releases her eggs, the male fertilizes them in the water. Millions of eggs form a raft and float to the surface. Once they hatch, the young swim back down to the sea depths.

Male angler-fish attach themselves to a female. They will feed off her for the rest of their lives.

SPERM WHALES

Huge sperm whales can dive deep into the bathypelagic zone. They swim rapidly through the water, chasing after squid. The whales will catch squid after squid, chewing their prey with the stubby teeth in their lower jaws.

Most deep-sea creatures get their oxygen from the water. Sperm whales are different—they breathe air. They can hold

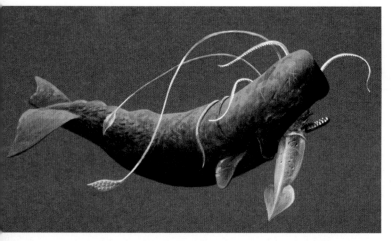

In this drawing, a sperm whale makes a meal of a giant squid, one of its favorite foods.

their breath for a long time, but they have to get back to the surface every hour or so. A sperm whale may have to swim up a whole mile (1.6 kilometers) to reach the surface. It bursts out of the water and takes a great steamy breath through the blowhole, or nostril, on top of its head. The whale doesn't stay at the surface long. It breathes in air for about fifteen minutes. Then it closes its blowhole and dives back down again.

If a scuba diver tried to swim to the surface as fast as a whale, he would become sick from the rapid change in water pressure. That's because, when a person inhales, some of the nitrogen in the air dissolves in his bloodstream. As the diver descends, the increasing water pressure squeezes more nitrogen into his body. If he rises too fast, the nitrogen comes out too quickly, forming dangerous bubbles in his blood vessels. A whale, however, can force the air from its lungs into its windpipe, so less nitrogen is absorbed in its blood. It can dive up and down quickly with no problem.

TUBE WORMS

A mile (1.6 kilometers) deep on the floor of the Pacific Ocean, masses of huge tube worms cluster around hydrothermal vents, swaying gently. With their long white bodies and red tips, they look like big, flexible lipsticks. In a place where there is no sunlight and the vents spew out hot bursts of **sulfur** chemicals, how do these creatures survive, let alone get so big?

Giant tube worms may grow to 7 feet (2 meters) or longer.

Tube worms have no mouths, eyes, or stomachs. Inside their bodies are tiny bacteria that turn the sulfur into food. The tube worms simply absorb the food that the bacteria create. How did the bacteria get inside these creatures in the first place? Scientists have discovered that early in their development, tube worms have a sort of mouth through which bacteria can enter. As the tube worms grow older, the mouth disappears, trapping the bacteria inside.

Most life on earth depends on photosynthesis, the process through which plants use sunlight to convert carbon dioxide and water into food. The hydrothermal vents are the only places we know of where life depends not on photosynthesis but on chemosynthesis. Deep down in the ocean, where there is no sunlight, sulfur chemicals are the basis for life. Through chemosynthesis, deep-sea creatures like the tube worms use bacteria to turn these chemicals into a constant and plentiful source of nutrients.

GIANT VENT CLAMS

Tube worms are not the only oversized creatures living around hydrothermal vents. Colonies of giant vent clams, as white as ghosts and as big as dinner plates, wedge themselves in the

cracks in the rocks. Imagine trying to eat a clam that big!

Actually, giant vent clams are no good to eat. They smell and taste like rotten eggs! Like tube worms, these creatures rely on tiny bacteria that convert smelly sulfur chemicals into food. The bacteria live not inside the clam's belly but on the gills on the side of its body. The gills extract oxygen from the water.

Unlike other clams, giant vent clams don't stay mostly in one place. They move about on their one large, fleshy foot, searching for the best conditions to grow their gill bacteria. These huge clams don't need to get together to reproduce. Instead, the male and female clams spew sperm and eggs into the water, and the free-floating sperm fertilize the eggs. When the larvae first hatch, they have no shells. They float about in the water for a few weeks. Then they settle to the bottom and begin growing their own huge shells.

Giant vent clams, as big as dinner plates, cluster in colonies near hot vents.

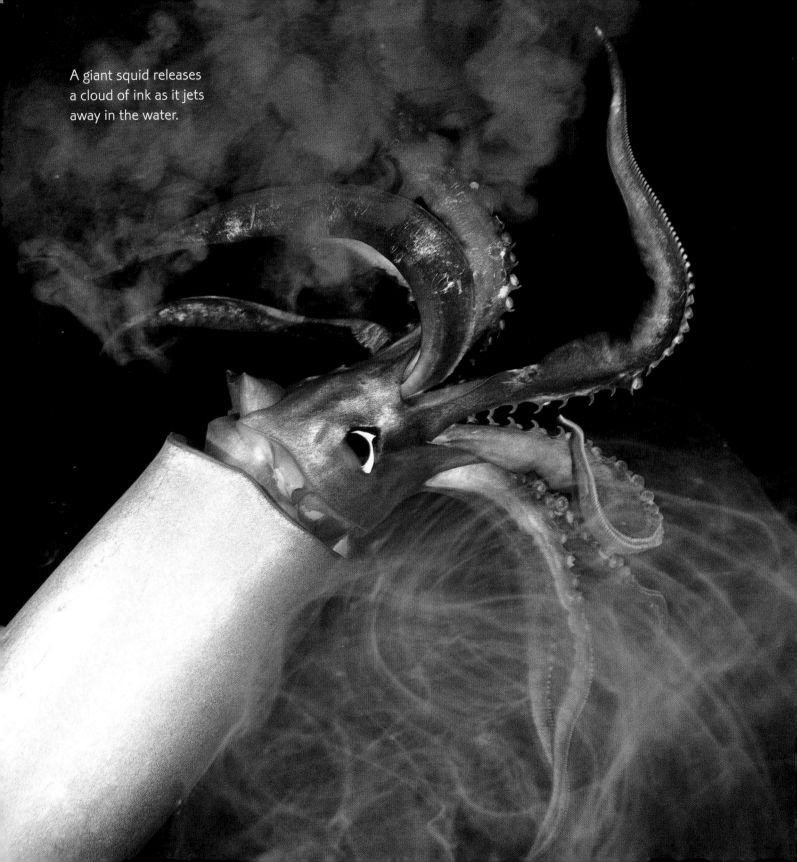

A giant squid releases a cloud of ink as it jets away in the water.

CREATURES OF THE
ABYSSOPELAGIC
ZONE

13,000 TO 20,000 FEET
(3,960 TO 6,100 METERS)

GIANT SQUID

FAR BELOW THE OCEAN'S surface, giant squid hunt for dinner. They move with tremendous speed, shooting backward and forward, searching for prey. A squid moves mostly by jet propulsion, drawing water into its body, then shooting the water out at great pressure through a tube-shaped muscle, or funnel, that lies under its head. It can rotate the funnel to jet forward, backward, or sideways.

These deep-sea creatures have eight arms and two long tentacles. A giant squid can catch a fish even from far away. It simply folds its tentacles back to its head, then shoots them forward. *Snap!* The squid grabs the fish in a flash. Rows of big suckers on the squid's arms and tentacles make escape impossible. The squid holds the fish tightly. It pushes the fish into its mouth and bites down with its razor-sharp beak. Then it chews its meal to a pulp with the teeth on its tongue.

A giant squid is truly a giant. Some of these creatures can grow as long as 46 feet (14 meters). Imagine

REALLY BIG

The giant squid is the second-largest invertebrate (animal without a backbone) in the world. The only larger invertebrate is its gigantic cousin the colossal squid. This is one of a giant squid's huge eyes.

seven basketball players standing on top of one another. Now that's a giant!

The giant squid is a lot smarter than you might think. It has a huge, complex brain that sits between its eyes and all around its throat. It also has incredibly large eyes and excellent eyesight. Besides all that, the squid has the largest nerve fibers of any animal, which gives it lightning-quick reflexes.

You would think that a creature this big, smart, and well armed wouldn't have any enemies. But sperm whales are not afraid to attack one of these giants. The squid can try to jet away from its attacker, or it may grab on with its tentacles and give the whale a fierce bite. It may even try holding the whale under the water until the whale drowns. Still, in a fight between a giant squid and a sperm whale, the whale usually wins.

DEEPWATER MEDUSAS

A jellyfish called the deepwater medusa is another oversized creature that inhabits the abyssopelagic zone. While most jellies

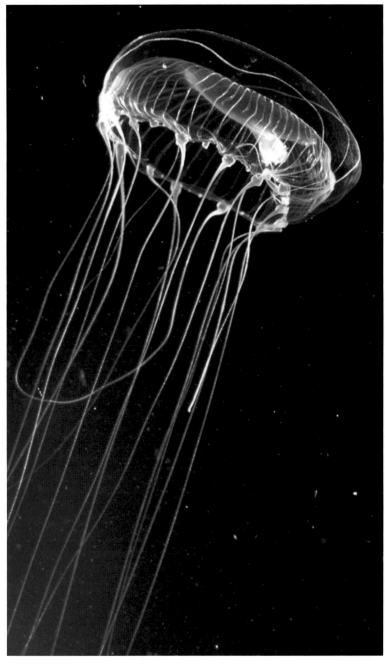
All jellyfish move by jet propulsion.

are no more than 6 inches (15 centimeters) across, the deepwater medusa may grow up to 20 inches (50 centimeters).

Like other jellyfish, the deepwater medusa moves by jet propulsion. As it pulses its strong muscles, it shoots out water, propelling itself along at quite a clip. The deepwater medusa carries its twelve stiff tentacles pointed upward as it moves about in search of small creatures living in the plankton. It snags its prey with its tentacles. It stings the victim with the stinging cells located on the tips of the tentacles. Then it bends its tentacles down to scoop the food into its mouth.

Even though deepwater medusas have stingers, they can't escape all predators. At night and in the winter, they sometimes migrate to shallower waters to feed. If one of these jellies gets too close to the ocean floor, a meat-eating creature called a sea anemone may lash out with its own tentacles. The medusa will pulse wildly, trying to escape, while the sea anemone slowly pulls its struggling victim into its mouth.

When the young of other jellies hatch, they go through several stages before they mature. But deepwater medusas go through a direct development from egg to maturity. This takes several months, and all that time the young don't eat. If they survive their predators, they may live up to thirty years.

Sea lilies wave
their feathery
arms deep down
in the hadal zone.

CREATURES OF THE HADAL ZONE

BELOW 20,000 FEET
(6,100 METERS)

SEA LILIES

IF YOU WERE EVER LUCKY enough to see a "garden" of sea lilies swaying in the ocean current, you would probably think these creatures were some kind of plant. Sea lilies are rooted to the rocks and have a stalk topped by what looks like a flower. But they are really animals. The "flower" is actually the creature's body, and the "petals" are its feathery arms.

Sea lilies are related to starfish, sea urchins, sea cucumbers, brittle stars, and feather stars. Like them, they have spiny skins and are radially symmetrical. That means that the animal's body parts are arranged around its center like the spokes of a wheel around the hub. A sea lily's mouth is in the center of its body. By waving its arms, it can filter tiny bits of food from the plankton. The food bits get trapped in **mucus** in grooves on its arms. Then the sea lily can push the food into its mouth.

Sea Cucumbers

Imagine seeing a herd of cucumbers trotting along the ocean floor! Striped sea cucumbers really do look like cucumbers from the vegetable garden. They have tubular projections called tube feet, with suckers on the tips that help them get a grip on surfaces. They rock from side to side as they move along. Sea cucumbers often travel together in herds in their search for food.

Although it has no head, a sea cucumber does have a mouth. The mouth is surrounded by a ring of tentacles. As the sea cucumber ambles along, it uses its tentacles to snatch food floating by and to search for tasty bits in the mud.

Top: A sea cucumber trots along the seafloor on its tube feet.
Bottom: In an effort to save itself, a sea cucumber shoots out its internal organs.

The sea cucumber has some other very odd features. For one thing, it breathes through its anus! It also has a strange way of protecting itself from predators. If a fish starts nibbling, the sea cucumber will suddenly shoot out its guts and other internal organs. The startled fish quickly swims off, and the sea cucumber goes on its way. Of course, if any other animal shot out its guts this way, it would die. But the sea cucumber can actually regrow its internal organs in a few weeks and live to feed again.

SEA SPIDERS

Spiders may be the last creatures you would expect to find deep down in the hadal zone. In truth, you won't find them here, since sea spiders aren't really spiders at all. With their small bodies and long, hinged legs, they certainly do look spidery. But they are only distantly related to land spiders, as well as horseshoe crabs, scorpions, and mites. Sea spiders are ancient creatures. Their earliest-known ancestors were roaming around 500 million years ago.

Most sea spiders are small, no more than a third of an inch (10 millimeters) across. There are exceptions, however. A red sea spider known as the marine spider is huge! It can grow nearly 3 feet (1 meter) across.

Unlike land spiders, sea spiders have no lungs or respiratory system. How do they breathe down there on the ocean floor? They simply absorb oxygen from the water directly into their bodies.

Sea spiders wander about the seafloor in search of their prey.

When one of these spidery creatures comes across a jellyfish, sea anemone, or other soft-bodied animal, it grabs on with a pair of fanglike mouth parts called chelicerae (kih-LIH-suh-ree). The sea spider starts shredding its prey to bits. Then it uses its long **proboscis** to suck up the juices.

A male sea spider carries around a ball of eggs, protecting them until they hatch.

Sea spiders have a strange way of reproducing. The male attaches himself to a female and releases sperm from a tube on his legs. At the same time, the female releases eggs from tubes on her legs. Then the male gathers the fertilized eggs into a ball and sticks them onto a special pair of legs called ovigers (OH-vuh-jerz). He keeps the eggs safe by carrying them around until they hatch.

There are so many amazing creatures down in the deep! Wouldn't you love to hop aboard a deep-sea vehicle and go see them for yourself?

Words to Know

atrophy To decrease in size or waste away, like a body part that is no longer used.

crustaceans Animals with an outer skeleton and a pair of legs on each body segment, which live mostly in the water. Lobsters, crabs, and shrimp, for example, are crustaceans.

degenerate To decline, or develop into an inferior form.

dredge An iron frame with a net attached, used for gathering animals at the bottom of the ocean.

hydrothermal vents Openings in the ocean floor that spew out hot, mineral-rich water.

larvae The young of many invertebrates (animals without backbones).

mucus A slimy fluid that protects parts of an animal's body. In humans, for example, mucus coats and protects the insides of the mouth, nose, and throat.

plankton Very small plants and animals that float in oceans, lakes, and rivers.

proboscis A slender, tubular feeding and sucking organ.

species A group of animals or plants that have many characteristics in common. Members of the same species can mate and bear offspring.

sulfur A yellow chemical element that occurs widely in nature, especially in volcanic areas. When sulfur is mixed with other elements, it can smell like rotten eggs.

tentacles Long, thin body parts on an animal that are used to feel, grasp, smell, and move.

Learning More

BOOKS

Jenkins, Steve. *Down Down Down: A Journey to the Bottom of the Sea.* Boston: Houghton Mifflin Books for Children, 2009.

McMillan, Beverly, and John A. Musick. *Oceans.* New York: Simon and Schuster Books for Young Readers, 2007.

Rice, A. L. *Deep Ocean.* Washington, DC: Smithsonian Institution Press, 2000.

INTERNET SITES

Dive and Discover: Expeditions to the Seafloor

www.divediscover.whoi.edu/

This site lets you follow along as researchers in the submersible vehicle *Alvin* explore the ocean floor.

Earth's Oceans: An Introduction

www.enchantedlearning.com/subjects/ocean/

This site has lots of information on life in the oceans.

Index

Page numbers for illustrations are in boldface